On Board The TITANIC

First published in the United States by
Hyperion Books for Children,
a division of The Walt Disney Company
114 Fifth Avenue
New York, N.Y. 10011-5690

12 11 10 9 8 7 6 5 4 3 2

Library of Congress Cataloging-in-Publication Data

Tanaka, Shelley.
On board the Titanic / by Shelley Tanaka.
"An I was there book."
First published in 1996 by Hyperion Books for Children.
Summary: Seventeen-year-old Jack Thayer explores the Titanic and forms a brief friendship with another passenger
before experiencing the wreck of the giant ocean liner.
ISBN 0-7868-0283-9 (case) ISBN 0-7868-1318-0 (pbk)
1. Titanic (Steamship) — Juvenile fiction.
(1. Titanic (Steamship) — Fiction. 2. Shipwrecks — Fiction. 3. Ocean liners — Fiction.)
I. Title
PZ7. T161350n 1996   (Fic) — dc20   95-49035 CIP AC

Design and Art Direction: Gordon Sibley Design Inc.
Maps and Diagrams: Jack McMaster
Editorial Director: Hugh M. Brewster
Project Editor: Ian R. Coutts
Editorial Assistance: Nan Froman
Production Director: Susan Barrable
Production Co-ordinator: Donna Chong
Color Separation: Colour Technologies
Printing and Binding: Artegrafica S.p.A.

On Board the Titanic was produced by Madison Press Books,
which is under the direction of Albert E. Cummings

Madison Press Books
40 Madison Avenue
Toronto, Ontario
Canada M5R 2S1

Printed in Italy

Previous page: Passengers were given this postcard, showing the *Titanic* at full steam, on board the liner.
Right: The *Titanic* just before the fatal collision with an iceberg.

ON BOARD THE TITANIC

An I WAS THERE Book

What it was like when the great liner sank

TITANIC

BY SHELLEY TANAKA
PAINTINGS BY KEN MARSCHALL

A HYPERION/MADISON PRESS BOOK

Jack Thayer stared up from the pier at the gleaming black side of the *Titanic*. If he craned his neck he could just see the top of one of the ship's four huge funnels.

All morning he had been listening to people talk about the world's biggest ship. He was tired of hearing how brand, spanking new she was, the most luxurious ocean liner ever built. He was just glad to be going back to America after months of traveling in Europe with his parents. But as he got closer to the *Titanic*, he began to walk more quickly. Perhaps going on the first voyage of this giant new ship would be exciting after all.

At the end of the covered gangway that led into the ship, a man in a green jacket offered him a white carnation. Jack was puzzled.

"For your buttonhole, sir," the steward said.

Jack took the flower and, fumbling, tried to put it in his lapel.

"Jack! Get a move on! Other people are waiting."

He turned to see his mother and father waving him ahead. Behind them other passengers were waiting to get on board. He stepped onto the thick carpets of a large white room lined with potted palms. Uniformed stewards were helping other passengers find their staterooms. In the middle of the reception room, a shiny candelabrum stood at the foot of a wide staircase with a curving handrail. Before long, a steward was ushering the Thayers up this staircase toward their rooms on C-deck.

Inside their suite the smell of fresh paint still lingered, and Mrs. Thayer asked the steward to open the portholes. Porters then arrived with their luggage, and his parents began supervising the unpacking. Jack thought this would be a good time to make his escape and explore the ship.

"I'm going to have a look around, Mother. I'll see you both later."

"Just a minute, young man," said his mother, turning away from where

Jack Thayer.
(Left) The *Titanic* at the pier in Southampton, England.

her maid was unpacking dresses carefully wrapped in tissue paper. "This is a very big ship. Are you sure you won't get lost?"

Jack's father poked his head around the doorway. "The boy is seventeen years old, Marian. If he gets lost, he can ask for help. There are more stewards on this ship than ants at a picnic." Mr. Thayer turned to Jack and winked. "You go ahead, son, but meet us in the reception room in an hour."

Jack gave his father a wave and hurried off. He thought he would start at the top of the ship and work his way down. As he climbed the Grand Staircase, a shaft of sunlight poked through the large glass dome overhead. Thinking he might take a walk on deck, he followed a group of people who seemed headed in that direction. Instead he found himself in the ship's gymnasium, where an instructor in white trousers was urging people to try out the exercise machines. Two people pedaled stationary bicycles, and a man with a large mustache grinned as he bumped up and down on a leather-covered machine that imitated a horse ride.

Jack decided to see if he could find the swimming pool he had heard people talking about. He saw an open elevator and stepped inside.

"Say," he said to the elevator operator, "isn't there

Near the top of the forward Grand Staircase (left) was the ship's gymnasium (right) with rowing machines, stationary bicycles and even a mechanical horse (above).

supposed to be a pool on this ship?"

The operator turned around, and Jack saw that he was about his own age.

"The swimming bath, sir?" he replied in an English accent. "It's on F-deck. I can take you down to E-deck and it's down one flight from there."

After exploring the lower decks, Jack finally found the swimming pool but was disappointed to see that it was empty.

"We'll fill it later."

Thomas Andrews

The speaker behind him was a young-looking man in a brown suit with a pencil behind his ear and a roll of paper under his arm.

"Once we're out at sea," the man said, "they'll fill the bath with clean seawater."

"Do you work here?" Jack asked.

"I helped design the *Titanic* in Belfast. My name is Thomas Andrews." The man offered his hand.

Jack shook it. "That's terrific. But isn't your job over now?" *(Continued on page 10)*

The Thayer family would dress up for dinner each evening and then take these elevators (left) down to the first-class dining saloon. As first-class passengers, they would also have enjoyed swimming in the *Titanic*'s pool. It was one of the first swimming pools ever to appear on an ocean liner.

How big was the Titanic?

The *Titanic* was well named, for she was indeed a titan or giant among ships. If placed on her end, at 882 feet (269 meters), she was even longer than the tallest buildings of her day (below). The ship's enormous black hull weighed more than 50,000 tons. Her nine decks made her as high as an eleven-story building, and she had four huge funnels on top of that. The *Titanic* was called a floating palace because her restaurants, reception rooms and staterooms were so luxurious. It was claimed that the watertight compartments in the hull made her almost unsinkable. Stowed in her hold (right) was enough food to feed a small town, including 40,000 fresh eggs, 7,000 heads of lettuce and 36,000 apples. To serve it the ship carried more than 57,000 plates, cups and bowls.

R. M. S.

Café Parisien

Verandah and Palm Court

Hospita

Poop deck

Propellers

Third-class cabins

Second-class cabins

Second-class dining saloon

Engine rooms

TITANIC

Compass platform

Whistles

Gymnasium

Wheelhouse

Crow's nest

First-class lounge

Bridge

Wireless room

Third-class cabins

First-class staterooms

First-class dining saloon

Grand Staircase

First-class staterooms

Morse lamp

Turkish baths

Swimming pool

Boiler rooms

First-class promenade

Reception room

The Café Parisien (above) provided drinks and snacks at almost any time of day. The reception room (below) was where people gathered before and after dinner.

Andrews smiled. "Far from it. We're always making changes and improvements." He quickly scribbled a note and stuffed it in the pocket of his jacket. "Well, I've got more inspections to make. You're welcome to come along, if you like."

It was all Jack could do to keep up as he followed Andrews through the ship, up and down steep ladders and along narrow passageways. One moment he was shivering in a cold room filled with thousands of fresh flowers. The next minute he was watching as Andrews put his head inside a large machine that scrubbed and peeled potatoes.

Looking at his watch, Jack suddenly realized that he was late for meeting his parents in the reception room. As he rushed back, he ducked into the Café Parisien, one of the five restaurants on board the ship. It looked just like a French sidewalk café, with wicker chairs and real ivy growing up the walls.

The crowds that had filled the first-class reception room earlier were gone now. Instead, small groups of people sat at tables scattered around the room. The air was filled with the buzz of many people talking, and the ship's band played quietly in the background.

"Here we are, dear," Mrs. Thayer called out, waving to Jack over a potted palm. Jack's parents were sitting with a group of familiar people. He recognized Mr. and Mrs. Widener and their son, Harry, who lived near the Thayers outside Philadelphia. Mr. Widener, who had made his fortune building streetcars, was one of the richest men on board.

Jack's parents, Marian and John Thayer (above middle and right), and their friend George Widener (left).

Next to them sat Mr. and Mrs. Carter, who had a brand-new French car stored in the *Titanic*'s hold. Mr. Carter was fussing about the car as if it were a prize racehorse.

The grown-ups chatted nonstop, comparing the way their staterooms were decorated, or reading the names of well-known people from the printed list of first-class passengers. Many rich and famous people had paid huge amounts of money to sail on the first voyage of the most luxurious ship in the world.

Jack wasn't paying attention. He preferred watching the other people in the room. One woman had a fluffy object tucked under her arm. At first Jack thought it was her purse, but suddenly it moved and showed two beady little black eyes. The tiny long-haired dog and his mistress wore matching beaded collars.

Jack jumped as the *Titanic*'s whistle blew. All at once the group stood up. Everyone wanted to be on deck to watch the ship cast off.

THE DOGS ON THE TITANIC

The *Titanic* had dog kennels for the passengers' pets, and a crewman was assigned the task of taking the animals for a walk each day. As the ship sank, one passenger struggling in the water was very surprised when he came face to face with a bull dog. He later discovered that another passenger had gone to the kennels and released the dogs so that they wouldn't be trapped in their cages as the ship went down. Only two dogs survived the sinking, their owners managing to bring them into lifeboats.

Slowly and steadily the *Titanic* pulled away from the dock. From the shore a crowd waved and followed the ship along the pier. Jack noticed that people were tossing flowers from the ship. Suddenly he remembered the carnation in his lapel. Leaning over the railing, he threw it way down into the water.

Along the pier, several smaller ships were tied up. As the *Titanic* began to sweep past them, the suction from the big ship pulled a ship called the *New York* toward it. Several sharp cracks split the air like gunshots as the *New York*'s thick ropes snapped. The torn ropes whipped back toward the dock, right into the faces of the crowd.

The stern of the *New York* began to swing out. It was drifting right into the *Titanic*'s path.

Jack gripped the railing. He stared as the *Titanic* moved closer and closer to the *New York*. It was like watching a golf ball rolling slowly toward the hole. Would it miss? He held his breath.

At the last second, a tugboat appeared and began

to pull the smaller ship away. With only inches to spare, the *Titanic* slipped by the *New York*.

"Did you see that, Father?" Jack exclaimed. "That was a close one!"

There was no reply. When Jack turned his head, he saw that his father had moved down the railing to take photographs. In his place stood an elderly man, smoking a pipe.

The man frowned at Jack and shook his head. "Too close, if you ask me," he said. "It's bad luck for something like this to happen at the start of a maiden voyage."

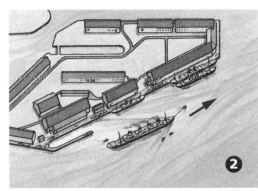

A Near Collision

A near accident occured just after the *Titanic* left her berth (painting opposite). The first diagram shows the huge ship moving slowly out of port ❶. As the *Titanic* sails down the narrow channel, she approaches two ships, the *Oceanic* and the *New York*, moored along the dock ❷. Pulled by the suction from the passing *Titanic*, the ropes holding the *New York* suddenly snap, and her stern swings out toward the huge ship. Luckily a nearby tugboat manages to attach a line to the *New York* to pull her back ❸. The *Titanic* reverses her engines to avoid a collision (photo above), and tugboats ❹ pull the *New York* away.

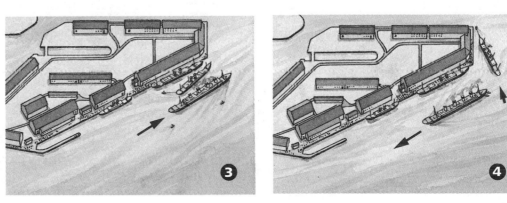

Harold Bride tiptoed up the *Titanic*'s Grand Staircase. He glanced at the large clock on the landing. It was 1:45 A.M., almost time for him to go on duty in the wireless room. His boss and friend, Jack Phillips, would be tired. Between them, the two men made sure the ship's wireless sent and received telegram messages twenty-four hours a day.

Harold looked around. He wasn't really supposed to be here, but at this late hour there was no one to notice. Besides, he wanted to see some of the fancy parts of the ship. As a junior wireless operator, he spent almost all his time working in the tiny wireless room or sleeping in the small bunk beside it.

Harold stared at the carved wood and the statues on either side of the clock. He wanted to touch them, to feel the polished banister, but his hands were full. The tray in his right hand was getting heavy. So was the bucket in his left.

Up on the boat deck, Harold carefully opened the door to the wireless room. Phillips's head was bent in concentration as he listened to messages through his earphones.

Harold put the tray quietly on a table. He shifted the bucket to his other hand and slowly crept up behind Phillips. Then, with a cry of "Happy birthday," he poured the bucketful of ice cubes down Phillips's back. Phillips roared and from his chair tried to take a swipe at Harold.

Later, as the two friends ate the pastries Harold had brought on his tray from the first-class dining room, Harold thought about how lucky he was. He worked with Jack Phillips, the funniest, most hard-working man he had ever known. And at the age of twenty-two, he had a job on the *Titanic*, the greatest passenger ship in the entire world.

The elegant Grand Staircase with its glass dome overhead (left) was the showpiece of the ship. A photograph of Harold Bride (above).

15

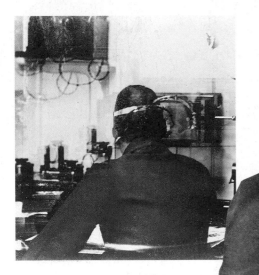

First wireless operator, Jack Phillips (right). His assistant, Harold Bride, is shown at work in the *Titanic*'s radio room (above). The drawing below shows a shipboard wireless operator sending out a message. The operators sent and received passengers' messages as well as information which helped direct the ship's course.

As Harold Bride stepped into the wheelhouse, he saw blue-uniformed officers pacing back and forth, scanning the sea ahead. With his white beard and square shoulders, Captain Smith was easy to spot. He just looked like the captain of a big, important ship.

"Sir, another ice message," Harold said, as he approached the captain. "From the *Baltic* this time."

"Thank you, Bride." The captain nodded and put the piece of paper in his pocket.

Harold walked back down the narrow corridor to the wireless room. He stuck his head out the door leading to the officers' promenade and took a few gulps of fresh air. From the decks below he could hear music and laughing and the clink of dishes. Those wealthy passengers in first class seemed to have nothing to do all day but stroll the decks and eat fabulous meals.

And send telegrams. It seemed that every first-class passenger on board wanted to send out greetings from the *Titanic*. Yesterday the wireless

On the Titanic's Bridge

C aptain Edward J. Smith (above) and his officers commanded the *Titanic* from the bridge.

1 The telemotor steering control and the ship's wheel.

2 The compass, used for finding the ship's direction.

3 A telegraph that sent messages to the engine rooms.

4 An additional wheel used to steer the ship.

5 The telephone picked up by one of the officers when the lookout announced that an iceberg lay directly ahead.

6 A telegraph used while docking.

17

had broken down. Phillips had been up all night repairing it. Now they were struggling to transmit all the messages that had piled up on their desk. Messages were coming in too. Their clicks and clacks would blast into their earphones just when Harold and Phillips were trying to send out their own messages. It could be very nerve-racking.

"Still busy?" Harold asked as he walked into the wireless room.

"Another iceberg warning." Phillips was scribbling furiously. "This one's from the *Amerika*." He took off his headset and scratched his ears.

"Are the icebergs dangerous?" Harold asked.

Phillips shook his head. "They might slow us down a bit, but they can't hurt a big ship like this."

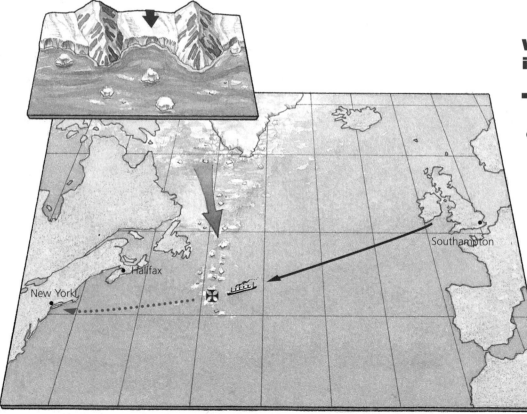

New York

Halifax

Southampton

Where did the iceberg come from?

The iceberg that collided with the *Titanic* in the North Atlantic Ocean most likely came from Greenland. Warm weather causes huge chunks of ice to break off Greenland's many glaciers (see inset left). These icebergs, along with smaller bergs and sea ice, float southward in the ocean. Sometimes they come together to form a pack of ice. Such an ice pack lay directly ahead of the *Titanic*.

Ships crossing the ocean in the spring would take a more southerly route than at other times of the year to avoid icebergs, then they would proceed due west toward New York. Because of the many ice warnings he received, Captain Smith sailed even farther south than usual. But he did not lower the speed of the ship, and by the time the lookout spotted the iceberg, it was too late.

The sun warmed Jack's face as he gazed over the railing at the calm, blue Atlantic. His mother and Mrs. Widener sat in deck chairs beside him, their legs wrapped in green plaid blankets.

After four days, Jack felt that he had finally explored the whole ship. He had been in the pool every day and had even tried out the Turkish bath. He had played squash. He had eaten two desserts at every meal. While exploring, he had run into Mr. Andrews a few times too. In fact, it almost seemed he couldn't turn a corner or walk down a staircase without finding the cheerful Irishman.

Mrs. Thayer tucked her deck blanket around her knees. "Brrr. It's getting very cold."

Jack saw that Mr. Ismay, the president of the White Star Line, which owned the *Titanic*, had joined them. "As a matter of fact, the captain handed me a telegram earlier," Mr. Ismay said. "We're near ice." He took a piece of paper out of his pocket and waved it at the ladies. "We should reach it this evening."

"Ice in April?" Jack asked. "Does this mean we won't arrive in New York on schedule?"

"Not at all," Mr. Ismay said. "We're making excellent time. A record run yesterday. We're going to start up some new boilers this evening. In fact, I expect we'll reach New York early and surprise everyone."

After dinner, Jack sat alone at a small table outside the first-class dining room. He was waiting for the band to begin playing.

His parents had gone to a special dinner party for Captain Smith in the fancy Ritz restaurant. Jack had eaten by himself, but he wasn't really disappointed. It was hard work making conversation with adults all the time.

"Excuse me, but could I use one of your matches?" A young man was pointing to the box on Jack's table.

The man's name was Milton Long, and he was traveling alone. Soon he and Jack were deep in conversation. Milton collected stamps, just like Jack. He loved baseball and parties. Now he was on his way home from Switzerland.

"I love to ski," he said. "But my father thinks it's too dangerous. Ever since I was shipwrecked near Alaska, he worries about me when I'm away."

"Shipwrecked?" Jack asked. "How were you rescued?"

"Oh, it wasn't difficult. We were only a few feet from shore at the time. I jumped from the boat onto the rocks. Only got my feet wet."

Jack laughed. It was good to talk to someone closer to his own age.

"Speaking of fussy parents, I'd better get back to my room," Jack said, checking his watch. "My mother will think I've fallen overboard."

"I'll see you tomorrow, then."

"Right." Jack waved happily. At least the last few days of the voyage would be more interesting now that he had made a friend.

SUNDAY, APRIL 14, 1912, 11:30 P.M.

**I**nside his stateroom, Jack pulled on his pajamas. Through the closed door he could hear his mother still talking excitedly about her dinner with the captain.

He opened his window a bit and looked out. The black sky hung over the ship like a magician's cape studded with diamonds. Jack had never seen so many stars.

There was a frosty chill in the air. All around him he could feel the soft, steady sound of the *Titanic*'s engines churning from below.

Jack wound his watch. It was 11:40 P.M. He pulled down the crisp white sheets of his bed and turned out the light.

Just as he began to climb into bed, the ship swayed slightly, as if it had been nudged gently on the shoulder. The movement was so small that Jack almost thought he had imagined it.

Then the engines stopped. After feeling their gentle hum under his feet for four days, the silence seemed very peculiar. It was like being on a slow-moving train that had suddenly come to a quiet stop. For several seconds Jack could hear nothing but the faint whistle of the breeze coming through his porthole.

Then he heard running footsteps and muffled voices out in the hallway. The ship's engines started up again in a slow, tired way. A moment later, they stopped for good.

Something was definitely going on. Jack pulled a heavy coat over his pajamas and shoved his feet into slippers.

"I'm going out on deck to see the fun," he called to his parents.

"I'm putting on my clothes now, son," Mr. Thayer replied. "I'll be right up to join you."

Outside on the promenade deck, it was very cold — so cold that Jack could see the puffs of his breath. On a lower deck were a few boys from third class, kicking something around on the deck. It almost looked like a piece of ice.

"Is that you, Jack?" Mr. Thayer hurried out on deck. "One of the crewmen says we've hit an iceberg. Can you believe it?"

Jack squinted out into the black night. Iceberg? He couldn't see anything.

He and his father walked upstairs to the first-class lounge. Several passengers stood around looking puzzled.

Up ahead, Jack saw Mr. Andrews.

"Let's ask him," Jack said. "He'll know what's going on."

Mr. Andrews spoke in a low voice. "We have struck an iceberg. I'm afraid that the ship has not much more than an hour to live."

Jack and his father looked at each other in disbelief. Then, without a word, they returned to their rooms. Mrs. Thayer and her maid were already dressed. Jack put on two vests, a suit and a coat. Then he tied on his bulky life jacket. He

The Fatal Collision

Shortly after 11:30 P.M., the *Titanic* was steaming along at high speed when one of the ship's lookouts spotted a large dark object looming in their path. "Iceberg right ahead," he shouted into the telephone to the bridge. The first officer immediately ordered the ship's engines to be reversed and her wheel turned as far as it would go to avoid the mountain of ice ❶. But seconds later there was a strange scraping sound. The iceberg had hit the side of the ship ❷ and ❸. The iceberg scraped against the *Titanic*'s hull plates, popping the steel rivets holding the plates together and allowing water to pour into the ship ❹.

put his overcoat on top.

Back outside, other passengers were gathering. Some people had put on several layers of clothes and life jackets, like the Thayers. Others wore their pajamas or bathrobes. A few women were still wearing evening dresses.

Somewhere on deck, the band began to play lively dance music. Above the ship, distress rockets shot up into the sky and burst into colored balls like fireworks. It was almost like being at a party, except nobody talked much.

"Jack!" It was Milton Long. He rushed up to the Thayers like an old friend.

"You haven't organized another shipwreck for our amusement, have you?" Jack said.

Milton shook his head, but he wasn't smiling. He

1 Deep inside the *Titanic*, in the boiler room nearest the bow, stokers were shoveling coal into the giant boilers. Suddenly water began to pour in from the side of the ship, nearly knocking them off their feet.

2 The stokers ran through the closing watertight door, which was operated by a switch on the bridge. But they found water pouring into the next boiler room as well and headed for higher decks.

3 The mail room was also filling with water. Clerks tried to move sacks of mail up to the post office, but soon it, too, was flooded, with stray parcels and letters floating about.

4 The iceberg scraped against six of the *Titanic*'s "watertight" compartments. They filled with water and, since they were not sealed at the top, water easily spilled from one to the next, ensuring that the *Titanic* would eventually sink.

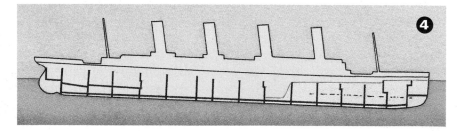

glanced at Mrs. Thayer. "They're loading the women and children into lifeboats. You'd better come."

Harold Bride rubbed his eyes tiredly. He had been asleep for a few hours, but Jack Phillips had been at the wireless desk all day. It was time to give his friend a break.

As he walked into the wireless room, Harold noticed how quiet the ship was. Phillips was still working, busily sending messages and taking down ice reports.

Then the door to the wireless room opened. It was the captain.

"Men, we've hit an iceberg. I'm having the damage inspected right now. Get ready to send out the call for

One hour after the *Titanic* hit the iceberg, Captain Smith ordered distress rockets to be sent off. He could see the lights of a ship in the distance, and hoped that the rockets would attract its attention. But the ship never responded. By this time the *Titanic*'s bow was sinking into the water. Even so, the ship's band continued to play for the passengers. In the end, none of the musicians survived.

Sending Out the SOS Call

In the *Titanic*'s radio room, Jack Phillips and Harold Bride used Morse code to send and receive messages over the radio. Morse code is a system of dots and dashes which represent the letters of the alphabet as well as each number (below). Messages in Morse code can also be sent by flashing a lamp. When the ship was sinking, Harold Bride suggested they send out SOS — three dots followed by three dashes, then three dots again. SOS had recently been chosen as an international distress call because it was easy to send and to recognize. It doesn't stand for "Save Our Ship," as some believe.

A	• —	J	• — — —	R	• — •	1	• — — — —
B	— • • •	K	— • —	S	• • •	2	• • — — —
C	— • — •	L	• — • •	T	—	3	• • • — —
D	— • •	M	— —	U	• • —	4	• • • • —
E	•	N	— •	V	• • • —	5	• • • • •
F	• • — •	O	— — —	W	• — —	6	— • • • •
G	— — •	P	• — — •	X	— • • —	7	— — • • •
H	• • • •	Q	— — • —	Y	— • — —	8	— — — • •
I	• •			Z	— — • •	9	— — — — •
						0	— — — — —

assistance, but don't do it until I tell you."

Phillips turned to Harold. "Well, mate," he said. "Looks like you'll see your first iceberg."

"At least the Americans will enjoy it. They all like to have ice in their drinks."

The two were still joking when a grim-looking Captain Smith returned.

"Send out the call for assistance," he said.

Without a word, Phillips started rapping out the call for help, over and over again.

"What are you sending?" Captain Smith asked when he returned a few minutes later.

"CQD," Phillips replied, as he continued to tap out the Morse-code distress call.

"Send SOS," Harold suggested. "It's the new call and it may be your last chance to send it."

It seemed like ages before Phillips turned around.

"I've got the *Carpathia*," he said. "She's on her way." He looked at Harold and grinned. "By the way, old man, do you want to be dressed like that when the rescue boats get here?"

Harold looked down. He was still in his pajamas. He hurried into the bunk room to change. Everything was going to be all right. Help was on the way.

For the next hour Harold stood beside Phillips.

As various ships answered the *Titanic*'s call for help, he would grab the message and take it to the captain. Each time he ran to the bridge, the deck seemed to slant down a little more.

At one point Phillips went out to have a look around. When he came back, his expression was grim.

"She's halfway under water," he said, his voice quavering. Harold looked at his friend's pale face. For the first time, he felt afraid. He knew that at least one ship was on its way. But would it reach the *Titanic* in time?

Harold went into the bunk room. He fetched warm clothes and life jackets. As Phillips continued to send out the call for help and listen for replies, Harold put a coat and life jacket on his friend.

"Power is getting weaker," Phillips muttered. "I can hardly hear a thing."

Passengers hurry up the first-class staircase to the lifeboats as water floods the landing five decks below them.

Jack Thayer and Milton Long stood together on the *Titanic*'s deck. The stern of the ship was tilted up out of the sea. The bow was covered with water, and inch by inch it crept higher and higher.

Nearby, hundreds of people watched the lifeboats being loaded. Most were men, who stood talking or smoking quietly. But there were some women, too, who refused to leave the *Titanic* without their husbands.

There was not much noise. Jack watched a father say goodbye to his two young sons. He kissed the older boy before thrusting him into the arms of a sailor who was waiting in a lifeboat. Thick ropes began to lower the boat to the sea. First one end lurched down, then the other. Then the father picked

The first lifeboats leave the ship (above), and later, the bow sinks lower and lower into the water (opposite).

up the smaller boy. He was so bundled up that he could hardly move. The man hugged his son and dropped him into the arms of a passenger in the boat. When he stepped back into the crowd, his face was so sad that Jack couldn't bear to look at it.

Another boat close by was already loaded with women and children. But the boat was too full. An officer said that one of the passengers would have to get out. A young woman stepped quickly out of the boat before anyone could stop her. Jack heard her voice clearly. "You are married and have families," she said firmly. "I'm not. It doesn't matter about me." Then she walked calmly away.

THE SHIP ON THE HORIZON

As the *Titanic* was sinking, the lights of another ship were seen in the distance. It may have been the *Californian*, which saw the rockets sent up by the *Titanic*. Officers on the *Californian* tried to signal the *Titanic* with their flashing Morse lamp, but they did not wake up their radio operator to listen for a distress call. The captain was later criticized for not going to the *Titanic*'s rescue.

KEN MARSCHALL 198?

Several boats already sat in the water a short distance from the ship. Jack tried to see whether his mother and father were in one of them, but it was too dark. In the crush of the crowd, he had lost sight of them as they led Mrs. Thayer to the boats.

"Should we try to get in a boat?" he asked Milton. He knew they were supposed to wait until all the women and children were safely off the ship. But

Jack had seen that a number of men, including Mr. Ismay, had managed to get away.

Milton pointed to a group of white-coated bellboys and elevator boys standing quietly together. "If those fellows are waiting, then we should too."

Jack nodded. Some of the boys looked very young.

"What on earth is going on there?" he said. Farther down the deck were a man in an evening

30

suit and an elderly steward. They seemed to be tangled up in a pile of deck chairs and rope.

"They're tying chairs together." As Milton said this, the old steward picked up a couple of chairs and heaved them overboard. The chairs floated gently on the glassy water.

Jack felt the back of his neck prickle with fear. What he had known in his heart for the past hour was suddenly very clear.

They would never get in a lifeboat. There simply weren't enough. The floating chairs were makeshift rafts. They would be something to grab on to when the time came to jump.

And that time was now. The ship lurched beneath them. The bow slowly began to slide into the water. From inside the ship came a rumbling sound, like the roar of an express train passing over a steel bridge.

Jack threw off his overcoat. He and Milton climbed up on the railing. In the background, the ship's orchestra was still playing.

"This is it, Jack," Milton said, holding out his hand.

"I'll be right with you," Jack said. He didn't want to say goodbye. "Good luck."

Milton let go. Then Jack, with a push of his arms, jumped into the sea.

Why weren't there enough lifeboats?

The *Titanic* had sixteen lifeboats and four collapsible boats — only room for just over half the 2,200 people on board. Regulations for the number of lifeboats required had not caught up with the size of the new ship. And the ship's owners couldn't imagine that, in case of accident, the *Titanic* wouldn't be able to float until rescue ships reached it.

Captain Smith ordered women and children to get into the lifeboats first. But many still thought that the *Titanic* was safer than a small lifeboat in the cold waters of the Atlantic Ocean. As a result, several lifeboats left the *Titanic* only half full (painting above).

The icy cold of the water went through his skin like a knife. The ocean pulled him down and down. Jack used every ounce of his strength to struggle back to the surface.

Then he swam as hard as he could away from the ship.

arold Bride stood beside Jack Phillips. The captain had told them to abandon ship, but Phillips was still at his post tapping out the SOS call.

Finally, they could do no more.

Harold dashed out on deck. A group of men were trying to launch one of the collapsible lifeboats. He rushed to join them and reached for an oarlock. Then a great wave rolled along the deck, sweeping him overboard.

Harold blinked. His hand was still holding on to the oarlock. But the collapsible was upside down, and he was trapped in the water underneath it.

He knew he must not breathe. Somehow he managed to dive and come up to the surface beside the boat.

Sputtering, he shook the water out of his eyes. Several men were already crouching on top of the overturned boat. Harold tried to tug himself up.

By 2:05 A.M. the propellers had risen above the water (opposite). Harold Bride joined a group of men trying to free a collapsible boat (above). When the bow plunged downward, a huge wave washed him overboard (below).

Jack Thayer pulled Harold Bride out of the water onto the overturned collapsible boat (above), which was crowded with survivors trying to stay afloat (below). They watched as the *Titanic* began her descent to the ocean bottom (opposite).

"Help me, please," he called out. A few men looked at him and then turned away. They were frightened. There were many people in the water. And they were all crying out for help.

"Here, take my hand," a voice said. A young man pulled him up. Then the men huddled together, wet and freezing. As they looked back at the ship, she looked like a huge black beast rearing up into the air. The bright lights from her portholes flashed like thousands of tiny eyes. Then they blinked and went out forever. Suddenly the great ship began to split in two. Her funnels spat out smoke and sparks in a final angry fury.

Then her huge propellers lurched high out of the water, and the mighty *Titanic* plunged into the icy sea.

MONDAY, APRIL 15, 1912,
3:30 A.M.

Jack Thayer squatted on the overturned collapsible lifeboat. About two dozen exhausted men were around him on the shifting capsized boat. He could hardly see their faces in the black night. But he knew from their talk that many had worked in the *Titanic*'s engine rooms. Jack could only imagine what it must

have been like to come up from the hot furnaces only to jump into the icy ocean.

Would any of them ever see their families and friends again?

He looked down. The man he had pulled out of the water was lying at his feet. His legs were twisted against the edge of the boat, covered with freezing water. Every now and then a wave washed over his face, making him choke and sputter.

Jack bent down. He put his arm around the man's shoulders and gently helped him sit up. He held him like that, letting the fellow lean against his knees.

"My name's Jack," he said, as the man looked at him gratefully.

"Harold Bride." The man winced as he tried to shift his legs. "What time do you suppose it is?"

Jack looked at his watch. It had stopped at 2:22 A.M. "I don't know," he said. "Almost four, maybe."

"We'll be rescued soon. The *Carpathia* is coming up as fast as she can. I'm a wireless operator. I was there when the message came in. She knows our position."

"Are you sure?" Jack hardly dared to believe it.

"I just hope I can make it off this boat when help gets here."

"Listen, friend," Jack said, a smile cracking his frozen face. "If you're right about the *Carpathia*, I'll carry you off myself."

As morning drew closer, the sea became rougher. Whenever a wave washed over the side, the boat tilted dangerously. Then everyone had to lean carefully in the same direction to bring it upright again.

Jack grew drowsy. His body felt like a stump of wood, and he

Before sinking, the *Titanic* split in two between her third and fourth funnels, making a great cracking sound.

could no longer feel his legs. He leaned heavily against the man beside him and closed his eyes. His feet began to slide off the slippery wet bottom.

"Look!" someone shouted.

On the horizon was a light. Jack stared. Was it just a bright star?

He blinked hard and looked again. Sure enough, the light was getting closer.

It was a ship. She was coming to the rescue.

 ake it easy with my friend here. His legs are in a bad way."

Jack helped Harold make his way forward. The lifeboat that had picked them up from the overturned collapsible was lashed

alongside the *Carpathia*. As Harold put his foot on the first step of the ladder, he paused. There in the bottom of the boat lay the lifeless body of someone who must have died during the night. Harold had an awful feeling that it was Jack Phillips. Without a word, he started to climb up the ladder.

It was Jack Thayer's turn. First he took off his life jacket, his frozen fingers fumbling with the ties. Then he climbed the rope ladder and felt the solid deck of the *Carpathia* under his feet. Nearby, Harold waved weakly from a stretcher as he was carried down to the ship's hospital.

The deck was crowded with people. A woman handed him a blanket. Someone else offered him a cup of hot soup.

Jack looked around. Where were his parents? He searched for a familiar face.

In the Lifeboats

Jack Thayer and Harold Bride clung onto the overturned collapsible boat, watching in horror as the huge ship vanished. Later, only two lifeboats returned to pull survivors from the water. The people in other boats feared they would be swamped by the hundreds struggling for their lives in the icy ocean. When their wailing stopped, an eerie calm took over. Many of the survivors watched shooting stars overhead. It was bitterly cold. In one boat a steward passed out handkerchiefs for passengers to put on as hats.

Several lifeboats tied up to one another and drifted together on the vast ocean. Women took charge of the oars in many boats. Jack Thayer's mother

rowed for five hours, her feet covered by water. In another lifeboat a woman waved her cane, which had a built-in electric light, to signal other boats. Around 3:30 A.M. the survivors heard a boom and spotted a light in the distance. It was the *Carpathia*, firing off rockets to reassure the survivors that help was on the way.

(Above) Packed full of survivors, one of the four collapsible boats nears the *Carpathia* (right). A crewman aboard the rescue ship watches as a rope ladder is lowered to survivors in one of the lifeboats (far right).

At first he saw only one. At the far end of the deck, a man was being led inside. It was Mr. Ismay. His face was pale, and his eyes stared ahead blankly as he stumbled to the door. He looked like a broken old man.

Jack remembered watching Mr. Ismay climb into one of the *Titanic*'s lifeboats while so many others stayed behind. What would become of him now?

"Jack!"

He looked up and ran to his mother.

"They said this was the last boat to come in. I was beginning to give up hope." She looked around desperately. "Where's your father?"

Jack's heart sank. He shook his head. Then he and his mother fell into each other's arms and cried.

MONDAY, APRIL 15, 1912,
6:00 P.M.

J ack Thayer walked along the upper deck of the *Carpathia*. The ship looked like a campground. The *Titanic*'s survivors were huddled in every corner of the deck and in every hallway. Others lined up for soup. The ship's dining room had been turned into a giant temporary bedroom. The survivors were dressed in whatever

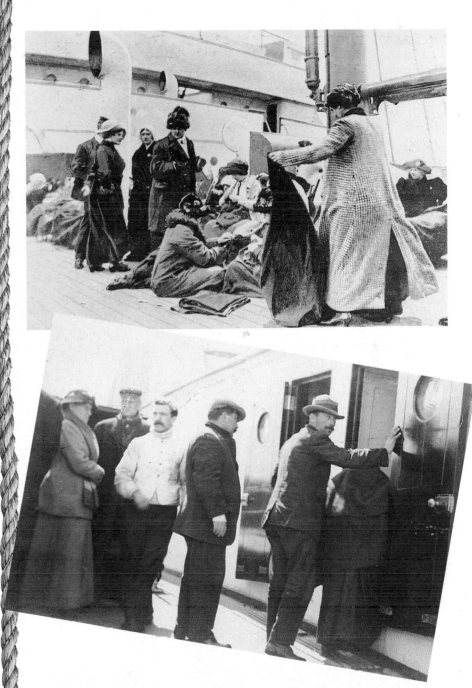

Passengers on the *Carpathia* gave clothing and blankets to the *Titanic* survivors (top), who can be seen (above) lining up for a meal.

clothing the *Carpathia*'s passengers and crew could spare. One small boy wore a lumpy nightgown made from a gray blanket.

At last Jack found the wireless room. It was located in a white wooden shack tucked behind the funnel. He opened the door. Harold Bride sat crouched over the desk.

Jack tapped Harold on the shoulder. The young wireless operator looked up. His face was drawn and there were dark circles under his eyes, but he smiled when he saw Jack.

"I can't believe you're working," Jack said. "Shouldn't you be in bed?"

"Well, the regular wireless man has been going without a break since yesterday morning. So they asked me to come up. No one else knows how to operate this thing, and there's a lot to do."

Harold pointed at the stack of messages and long lists of names in front of him.

"Besides," he said, "I was glad to help out. It's what Phillips would have done."

"Phillips?"

Titanic survivors comfort one another (left), and a three-year-old boy wears a nightshirt made from a blanket (above) on the *Carpathia*. His frozen feet wrapped in bandages, Harold Bride is carried off the rescue ship in New York (right).

"The other wireless man on the *Titanic*. Best mate I ever had. He didn't make it."

"No," replied Jack. "Neither did my father."

Jack looked down. So many had not survived. His friend Milton Long, Mr. Widener and Harry, Mr. Andrews and hundreds and hundreds of others.

"How are your legs and feet?" he asked quietly. Harold's bandaged feet stuck out in front of him like giant snowballs. They had been frozen.

Harold winced. "They hurt, all right. Some men had to carry me up here, but I can work propped in a chair. The newspapers keep sending messages, begging me to tell them about the sinking. They want to hear every horrible detail. Some have even offered money. But I think it's more important to send out the names of survivors to the families. It just seems like the right thing to do."

Jack nodded. "I'll leave you to it, then. I just wanted to see that you were all right. Good luck."

The two shook hands and Jack turned to go. When he looked back, Harold was already hard at work again. Jack knew he would never forget the sight of him.

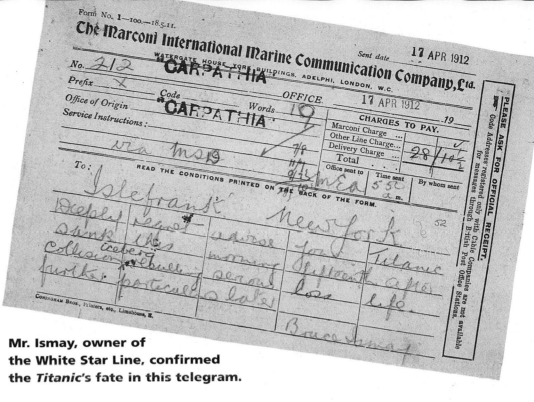

Mr. Ismay, owner of the White Star Line, confirmed the *Titanic*'s fate in this telegram.

He walked back out onto the deck. Small clusters of people sat huddled together sadly. They had all lost friends and family.

He spotted his mother standing by the rail and went and stood beside her.

"Oh, there you are, dear. Thank goodness. I hate to have you out of my sight for even a minute," she said, taking his arm.

Jack patted his mother's hand.

"Looks like we're finally heading out of the ice," he said.

Behind them the sea was dotted with icebergs glistening in the sun. It had taken the *Carpathia* all morning to make her way through the ice field. Then

Who died and who was saved?

First-class passengers

††ıllıllıllıllıllıllıllıllıllıllıllıllıllıllıllıll
ıllıllıllıllıllıllıllıllıllıllıllıllıllıllıllıllıllıllıllıllıllıllıllıllıllıllıllıllıllıllıllıll

††
†††††††††††††††††††††ıllıllıllıll

Second-class passengers

††††††††††††††††ıllıllıllıllıllıllıllıllıllıllıllıllıllıllıllıllıllıllıllıllıllıllıllıllıllıll
ıllıllıllıllıllıll

†††
†††††††††††††††††††††††††††††††ıllıllıllıllıllıllıll

Third-class passengers

††ıllıllıllıllıllıllıllıllıllıllıll
ıllıllıllıllıllıllıllıllıllıllıllıllıllıllıllıllıllıllıllıllıllıll

††
†††
†††
†††
†††††††††††††††††††††††††††††††††ıllıllıllıllıllıllıllıllıllıllıllıll
ıllıllıllıllıllıllıllıllıllıll

Crew

ıllıllıllıllıllıllıllıll††
††
†††††††††††††††

ıllıllıllı†††
††
††
††
††
††

The diagram above shows the many lives lost on the *Titanic* (the figures in black) compared to the few who were saved (the figures in red). By far the greatest number of those drowned were third-class passengers and crew.

(Right) A newsboy in London sells a paper with news of the disaster.

she had sailed alongside it all afternoon. Now she turned her bow to the west. In a few days she would arrive in New York City, where the whole world was waiting to hear about the *Titanic* disaster.

"It looks like a fairyland, doesn't it?" Mrs. Thayer said. "The ice sparkles like jewels."

As Mrs. Thayer leaned her head on her son's shoulder, Jack looked out over the vast ocean. The sun was sinking lower in the sky. Its rays were beginning to shine pink off the edge of the ice field that was slowly disappearing behind them.

He squeezed his mother's arm and pointed ahead of the ship.

"Look at that, Mother," he said. We're going to have a beautiful sunset."

EPILOGUE

fter the *Titanic* sank, everyone wanted to know what had gone wrong. Investigations were held in both the United States and England.

In the end, the experts decided that no one could be blamed for the sinking. But they also decided that sea travel should be safer. All ships should carry enough lifeboats for every person on board. Special ice patrols would warn ships about icebergs.

Harold Bride was an important witness at both investigations. When the *Carpathia* arrived in New York, he met the famous Mr. Marconi, the man who invented the wireless telegraph. He was also interviewed by a reporter, and his story appeared on the front page of the *New York Times* the next day. When he sailed back to England, his father met the ship, and Harold was extremely glad to be home. He lived the rest of his life quietly, working as a wireless operator during World War I, and later as a salesman.

The world was not kind to Bruce Ismay, the

How did the Titanic sink?

1 As the bow filled with water, the first funnel collapsed.

2 Unable to bear the strain of the stern in the air, the ship broke in two.

3 The stern stood upright in the ocean before plunging to the ocean floor.

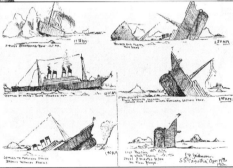

4 The bow of the ship glided to the bottom.

5 The ship's bow and stern landed nearly 2,000 feet (600 meters) apart. The inset, showing the *Titanic* breaking in two pieces, was drawn by a passenger on the *Carpathia* from Jack Thayer's description of the sinking.

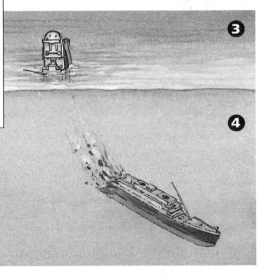

president of the company that owned the *Titanic*. Many felt he should have gone down with the ship, along with Captain Smith and more than 1,500 others. Thomas Andrews, in contrast, had helped people into the lifeboats right up to the end but had made no effort to save himself.

Jack Thayer went to university and had a successful banking career. He eventually married and had children. Eight days after the disaster, Jack wrote a long letter to Milton Long's mother and father, describing his short friendship with their son and what it had meant to him. Throughout his life, Jack insisted that he had seen the *Titanic* break in two on the night of the sinking. But experts thought it more likely that the ship had sunk in one piece. Jack was finally proved right in 1985, when Dr. Robert Ballard discovered the bow and stern sections lying nearly 2,000 feet (600 meters) apart on the floor of the Atlantic Ocean.

And Jack Phillips was not forgotten. People from around the world donated money to build a special memorial to him. Beside a little country church near Phillips's birthplace in England is a small garden. Ivy-covered walls surround a lily pond and a border of ferns and flowers.

The garden is a simple, green and peaceful place. It is a good place for thinking about the many, many brave people who were there on the night the *Titanic* went down.

Two and a half miles below the ocean surface, Robert Ballard explores the ghostly bow section of the *Titanic* wreck from his tiny submarine. He also examined the stern section of the ship and thousands of objects which were scattered nearby on the ocean floor.

GLOSSARY

aft: Toward the back of a ship.

boiler: A large coal-burning furnace that boiled water to create the steam which powered the ship.

bow: The front end of a ship.

bridge: The raised platform near the front end of a ship from which it is navigated.

candelabrum: A branched candlestick or lamp.

collapsible: A wooden-bottomed lifeboat with canvas sides which could be raised when the boat was in use or collapsed when it was stowed away.

forward: Toward the front of a ship.

funnels: The tall chimneys of a ship from which smoke escapes.

promenade: An upper deck on a ship where passengers may walk.

stern: The rear end of a ship.

steward: A person who takes care of passengers on a ship.

Turkish bath: A steam bath.

wireless: An early form of radio.

PICTURE CREDITS

All paintings are by Ken Marschall unless otherwise stated.

Front cover: (Top left) Illustrated London News (Bottom left) Don Lynch Collection (Top right) The Ulster Folk and Transport Museum (Bottom right) Southampton City Museums

Back cover: (Top right) University of Pennsylvania Archives (Bottom right) Illustrated London News

Front flap: Southampton City Museums

Endpapers: *The Sphere*, 1912

1: Ken Marschall Collection

3: Don Lynch Collection

5: University of Pennsylvania Archives

6: (Left) Library of Congress/ Ken Marschall Collection (Middle and right) Brown Brothers. Rope motif by Jack McMaster

7: (Top and bottom left) Ulster Folk and Transport Museum (Bottom right) Ken Marschall Collection

8: (Top left) Ken Marschall Collection (Top right) Diagram by Jack McMaster

10: (Top) Brown Brothers (Bottom) Library of Congress/Ken Marschall Collection

11: (Left) Brown Brothers (Middle and right) Don Lynch Collection

12: Dennis Faenza Collection

13: (Left) The Father Browne S.J. Collection (Right) Diagrams by Jack McMaster

14: Stanley Lehrer Collection

15: Illustrated London News

16: (Top and right) The Father Browne S.J. Collection (Bottom) Illustrated London News

17: Illustrated London News

18: Diagram by Jack McMaster

20-21: Don Lynch Collection

23: Michael Kohel Collection. Diagrams by Jack McMaster

24: Diagrams by Jack McMaster

25: Captain Ken Smith Collection

26: (Top) Diagram by Jack McMaster

30: Charles Heebner Collection

32: David Hobson Collection

33: Diagrams by Jack McMaster

34: Diagrams by Jack McMaster

40: (Left) National Archives/ Don Lynch Collection (Right) Brown Brothers (Bottom) Ken Marschall Collection

41: (Top) Mary Evans Picture Library (Bottom) Mr. George A. Fenwick Collection

42: (Left) Mary Evans Picture Library (Middle) Mrs. B. Hambly Collection (Right) Brown Brothers

43: J. Aidan Booth

44: (Left) Diagram by Jack McMaster (Right) Southampton City Museums

45: (Inset) Illustrated London News (Right) Diagrams by Jack McMaster

RECOMMENDED FURTHER READING

A Night to Remember
by Walter Lord 1955
(Bantam Books)
    The fascinating and detailed story of what happened the night the *Titanic* sank.

Polar the Titanic Bear
by Daisy Corning Stone Spedden, illustrated by Laurie McGaw 1994
(Little, Brown and Company, Canada, U.K., U.S.)
    Told through the eyes of a young boy's toy bear, the true story of an American family's travels in the Edwardian era, including their voyage on the *Titanic*.

Exploring the Titanic
by Robert D. Ballard 1988
(Penguin, Canada; Scholastic, U.K. and U.S.)
    The exciting story of how the *Titanic* sank and how she was discovered in 1985 on the ocean floor.

Titanic: An Illustrated History
by Don Lynch and Ken Marschall 1992
(Penguin Books, Canada; Hodder and Stoughton, U.K.; Hyperion, U.S.)
    A highly illustrated, in-depth account of the *Titanic* story and the people who sailed on the ship.

ACKNOWLEDGMENTS

Madison Press Books would like to thank Don Lynch and Ken Marschall for their expert historical advice. We are also grateful to J. Aidan Booth, Mr. George A. Fenwick, Mrs. B. Hambly and Terry Snyder, at the University of Pennsylvania Archives, for the use of photographs and to Ed Kamuda of the Titanic Historical Society (P.O. Box 51053, Indian Orchard, Massachusetts 01151-0053).